Evan[illegible]
Anglicans
and Liturgy

by

Colin Buchanan

Principal, St. John's College, Bramcote, Notts.
Member of the Church of England Liturgical Commission

GROVE BOOKS

BRAMCOTE NOTTS. NG9 3DS

CONTENTS

		Page
1.	Anglican Evangelicals	3
2.	Down to the 1960s	4
3.	Textual Revision	9
4.	Learning from Others	14
5.	Evangelical Initiatives	16
6.	Charismatics and Evangelicals	19
7.	The Group for Renewal Of Worship	20
	Appendix: The Two Statements	22

INTRODUCTION

'Tract no. 90' has been in view on the Group for Renewal Of Worship (G-R-O-W) for some time, and there has even been some jockeying to be author of the particular Booklet. The chairman put his foot down, and secured it himself. The Booklet does have a general survey role to it, and avowedly comes from an evangelical source and reflects on evangelicalism. (Only two previous titles have included the word 'evangelicals'—the second being Trevor Lloyd's commentary on the Nottingham Congress, No. 50, *Evangelicals, Obedience and Change*). Time and space have put both great limitations on this Booklet, but the series of incomplete vignettes may serve to provide a view of evangelicals emerging from their traditional liturgical ghetto and becoming interested in creatively using worship to build up the church of God. There is no space to debate here the merits of being liturgical persons in the first place (a recurrent evangelical question), and not much to indicate directions for the future. What there is is a measurement of ground covered, presented reasonably soberly. That may prove to be a good point of departure for the future. It is the English scene which is in view throughout.

Colin Buchanan

ACKNOWLEDGEMENTS

The Keele and Nottingham Statements are reprinted by kind permission of the Church Pastoral Aid Society, the proprietors of Falcon Publications. The cartoon in the cover pastiche is by Peter Ashton.

First Impression October 1984

ISSN 0144-1728

ISBN0 907536 79 4

1. ANGLICAN EVANGELICALS

Evangelicalism was at a low ebb in the Church of England in the first half of this century. That is not to say that evangelicals were lacking in faith, or short of piety, or uncaring about ministry. But it is to say that they were few in number, unproductive in theology, and defensive in relation to the rest of the Church of England. I have written about this elsewhere[1], and its effects in relation to liturgy are spelled out in the coming pages.

Since the Second World War, Anglican evangelicals have grown in numbers and in scholarship and in confidence. They have also become more volatile in character than previously, and the evangelicals of one generation are not necessarily like those of a previous one. As they have spilled out from their previous 'last-ditch' position, they have not only slowly shed their previous defensiveness and learned to take risks, but they have also, in the process, learned how to disagree with each other—sometimes charitably, sometimes not. If they have remained (by definition) those who treat the scriptures as supremely authoritative for the life and faith of the church, yet they have also discovered that the lessons of scripture cannot necessarily be 'read off' quite as easily as had sometimes been thought. And the escape from defensiveness has allowed evangelicals to become critical of their own 'traditions', not least their liturgical ones.

Whilst many landmarks could be picked out by which changes over the last twenty-five years could be charted, there have been three in particular to which I have made reference. These are:

(i) The First National Evangelical Anglican Congress held at Keele in April 1967. This is known as 'Keele', and the section of its 'Statement' which refers to worship is reprinted below on pages 22-23.

(ii) In 1972 John King edited for Lutterworth a book entitled *Evangelicals Today* (it was published in 1973), in which I wrote a chapter in January 1972 on 'Liturgy'. The book was called an exercise in 'Stock-taking', so that my chapter was deliberately intended to have that character.[2] I refer to it below as *Evangelicals Today.*

(iii) The Second 'NEAC' was held at Nottingham in April 1977. The relevant parts of its Statement are reprinted on pages 24-25 below, and it is referred to as 'Nottingham'.

For the rest, this booklet has to take for granted that readers know who Anglican evangelicals *are*—a task which is not always easy as numbers grow and hard distinctions blur.

[1] In particular, I would mention my articles on 'The Role and Calling of an Evangelical Theological College in the 1980's' in *Churchman* (Vol. 94 No. 1, February 1980) and 'Anglican Evangelicalism: the State of the "Party"' in *Anvil* (Vol. 1 No. 1, February 1984), both available as offprints from Grove Books.

[2] The blurb begins 'The one section of the contemporary Church that cannot be ignored is the Evangelical wing' and the back cover speaks of 'the most virile section of the contemporary Church'! It is a little triumphalist for my taste, and, I suspect, for the facts.

2. DOWN TO THE 1960s

The tradition of evangelicals was particularly defensive about the Book of Common Prayer. In fact, they had actually defended it successfully in 1927 and 1928. When all other schools of thought had put forward alternative proposals in the 1920s, the evangelicals, led by Bishop Edward Knox and Sir William Joynson-Hicks, had solidly refused to countenance alternatives, or be involved in making positive proposals.[1] And as the battle over the 1927 and 1928 'Deposited Books' narrowed down to a few sharp-edged questions about reservation of the sacramental elements and petitions for the departed, so their defensive stand paid off. They were among the few who recalled that the original terms of the Royal Commission of 1904-6 were the quest for a restoration of 'Ecclesiastical Discipline', and it was for a discipline that they stood and fought. This may have been wrong-headed. It may have included an element of cloud-cuckoo-land—in that neither accepting nor defeating the 'Deposited Book' was going to bring disciplines of the sort they wanted. It may have reinforced their Erastianism—for they had better hope of defeating the Book in Parliament than they had in the National Assembly of the Church of England. But they did get the Book defeated, and in general did thereafter insist it *had* been defeated when others were widely using it.

One has to acknowledge that in this back-to-the-wall fight they came across to others as harsh, uncompromising, and very like dogs in a manger. Gregory Dix, when discussing possible Prayer Book revision in 1945, wrote as follows:

> 'There is a section of the church, numbering perhaps a quarter of its members, the "Evangelical" party, whose set and fixed practice, if not principle, is opposition to the *recognition* of any sort of change in the *status quo* in the church. (They themselves have changed considerably both in teaching and practice since the time of Charles Simeon. It is not so much change as the acknowledgement of it that they dislike.) The nineteenth century bishops were so preoccupied with opposing the Oxford Movement that they took no steps to prevent what the Elizabethan bishops in their own day more wisely foresaw must be a danger to the cohesion of the church—the formation of a puritan *imperium in imperio* within the church, permanently

[1] '. . . the conservative Evangelicals, being for the most part satisfied with 1662, produced no proposals at all.' (*Prayer Book Revision in the Church of England: A Memorandum of the Church of England Liturgical Commission* (SPCK, 1957) p.10). But the undefensive Albert Mitchell *was* prepared to put forward a *ballon d'essai* after the 1928 fuss was over (see *The Churchman,* January 1929).

[2] It is arguable that the character of the official policy was to broaden the liturgical base of the Church of England, so as to include anglo-catholics and give legal status to mild forms of their practices, whilst setting clear limits so as to carry evangelicals for the changes: and what in fact went wrong was that each party got hold of the provisions made for the other and objected strongly—evangelicals to the broadening of the base, and anglo-catholics to the setting of limits! Yet Davidson could not promise evangelicals that anglo-catholics would conform, and thus had nothing to offer them at all—there was little or nothing in the contents of the 'Deposited Book' for them (cf. G. K. A. Bell *Randall Davidson: Archbishop of Canterbury* (Oxford,[3] 1952), p.1357).

impenetrable behind a financial rampart to any ideas current in the rest of the church. By the system of Evangelical schools, Evangelical halls at the Universities, Evangelical theological colleges and Evangelical patronage trusts, it is now quite possible for a boy to be educated and grow up, take a degree, be ordained and serve a ministerial lifetime, without once encountering directly any theological idea unacceptable to the founders of the party in the period of the Crimean War. To the framing of any new liturgy the Evangelicals would offer the most determined and conscientious opposition, not so much because they value the old one (which many of them disregard in different ways as flagrantly as any Anglo-catholic) as because it would mean admitting a change of some kind from what was customary a century ago. They would certainly decline to use any new liturgy which would satisfy the rest of the church, and they ought not in charity to be asked to do so. But this would not prevent their obstructing the official compilation of any new rite. The idea of composing a liturgy with the assistance and to the satisfaction of those who sincerely object to its coming into existence and who firmly intend never to use it is so Alice-in-Wonderland that it can hardly be discussed. But any proposal to be workable must bear this difficulty in mind.'[1]

There is an element of sheer truth about this. The more bizarre the deviations from the BCP of anglo-catholics, the more did evangelicals see their own place in the Church of England, and their own claim to be *the* true and loyal adherents to it, as bound up with the continuity of the unique place of the Prayer Book in the constitution of the Church. They took exactly the same view when they went overseas—all missionary work by evangelicals led to the use of the 1662 Book (translated into a vast number of languages)—whilst anglo-catholics took the opportunity to revise liturgical rites in a Romeward direction. And this in turn increased pressure upon evangelicals in England—the argument being that all revision in other parts of the world was all in one direction, and thus it was inevitable and right that England should follow![2] Evangelical resistance to change was consequently stepped up, and the conviction was deep upon them that all change was *bound* to be for the worse, and thus the very *principle* of change had to be resisted. Dix himself greatly assisted the pressures for change, because he exposed the Prayer Book communion rite for that which no anglo-catholic previously had ever so nakedly admitted it to be—a truly protestant and anti-catholic service, in total discontinuity with the pre-reformation uses.[3] He further increased the threat to evangelicals by avowedly

[1] G. Dix *The Shape of the Liturgy* (Dacre/Black, 1945) p.720.

[2] This argument only counted numbers of *rites*. It never counted numbers of *worshippers* using rites. The latter would have showed 1662 as ahead of all others put together until well into the late 1960s and perhaps even beyond (it is the staple use in Kenya and Uganda, for instance, to this day).

[3] Until his day most anglo-catholic writers viewed Cranmer's work as adequate though disjointed, a proof of the survival of catholicism through the reformation. Dix himself was opposed by, among others, Timms and Dugmore on just this point. But in fact he had blown the gaff on the issue, and nothing could now make plausible any suggestion it was *not blown*. (See Dix *op. cit.* pp.667-672).

renouncing legal or constitutional ways of proceeding towards revision, and favouring extra-parliamentary action![1]

At the same time, evangelicals can rightly feel misrepresented by what Dix said about them. It is only too easy to see them as clinging to the BCP on the grounds that it provided the right proof-texts to canonize their position in the Church of England, rather than because it was an apt vehicle for worship. A recent writer has lampooned evangelicals of the 1940s and 1950s as taking liturgy seriously only 'as a quarry for Protestant polemic or as proofs of impeccable doctinal rectitude'.[2] They might have appeared that way to others, but in their own parishes, they *used* the BCP. Yes, they really did. Their liturgical usage might, from Dix' point of view, have been frozen in time at around 1840 or 1850, but to them it was, in their own parishes, the natural (and far more biblical!) continuance with the reformed worship inherited from Cranmer. Cool it might be (passions were reserved for the sermon, and sometimes for the midweek prayer meeting, with just a touch of heartiness in the hymn-singing on Sundays), but tokenist or artificial it was not. It may well be true that evangelical congregations came in large part to hear the sermon (just as in most non-conformist churches), but they did really believe that the Prayer Book services were highly scriptural, were genuinely good for them, and ought to be conducted reverently by the ministers and followed carefully by the congregations.

Whilst certain characteristics of evangelical liturgical practice might have been distinctive, yet the commitment to the Prayer Book, however incomprehensible from Dix' standpoint, was not unique to them. The Church of England knew no official variant from the BCP until 1966.[3] The General Ordination Examination ran very strictly on Prayer Book lines—with great emphasis on the *text* of 1662—until well past that date. Hodder and Stoughton produced a wholly new series of 'The Prayer Book Commentaries' between 1961 and 1966. Even those parishes which took liberties with the communion service still played Morning and Evening Prayer fairly straight.[4] There still remained a general atmosphere in large parts of the Church of England that the Prayer Book was not only unchanged but also unchangeable.[5]

What was true was that to envangelicals this was important doctrinally, and the issue of 'polemics' *was* highly relevant (though, as noted, nothing like a wholly exhaustive statement of their view of the Prayer

[1] *op. cit.* pp.720-730.

[2] R. Buxton in K. W. Stevenson (ed.) *The Liturgy Reshaped* (S.P.C.K., 1982) pp.168-9.

[3] Not only so, the 1662 Book was built into the new Canons (A.5) and into the foundational doctrinal statement, parliamentarily entrenched, in the Church of England (Worship and Doctrine) Measure 1974 (section 5).

[4] It is observable that evangelicals tend to stick to the letter of communion services, whilst taking some liberties with Morning and Evening Prayer—whilst anglo-catholics have done just the opposite.

[51] Thus when the Liturgical Commission produced some draft rites for baptism and confirmation in 1959, and even demonstrated them round the country, no-one from the average parish could really persuade himself that these or other new rites were ever likely to *happen*.

Book). In the first documents relating to the foundation of Latimer House Jim Packer wrote in December 1958: 'The present situation is one of extreme urgency. Canon Law revision is in progress; Prayer Book revision is promised; revision of the Articles is threatened'.[1] Whilst the verbs used here about the Prayer Book and Articles differ, yet the context is the same 'extreme urgency'. The sense of being ecclesiastically in the last-ditch meant all hints of change to come were heard as threats (just as Dix had stated), and the general response was to gird oneself (as in 1928) to resist it. The Canon Law changes already going through were 'legalizing' stone altars, wafer bread, eucharistic vestments, and a variety of other uses evangelicals viewed as undermining the reformed character of the Church of England. The claim to be not only the true inheritors of the reformation settlement, but the truly constitutionalist, in the sense of being the sole keepers of the rules, was being severely threatened.[2]

Meanwhile, another threat to evangelicals was stealing up on them from all directions—the Parish Communion. Whilst the advocates of this claimed to represent all shades of churchmanship, the realities (to evangelical eyes) were far otherwise. Whilst there is no systematic body of *writings* directed against the encroachments of this pattern in the 1950s, yet the reasons for evangelicals' suspicions are not hard to find. They can be listed as follows:

(i) the pattern makes frequent reception of communion a panacea for all spiritual ills—healing wounds 'slightly'.

(ii) experience showed that the more successful a parish communion might be, the longer the administration would take.[3] This meant that the only way to save time was to trim down the sermon, and evangelicals became very scornful of seven-minute 'sermonettes'.

(iii) experience also showed that the sanction 'The Lord's Service for the Lord's People on the Lord's Day' tended to drive all worshippers toward the morning communion—and whereas prior to the Parish Communion the 'oncers' split evenly between mornings and evenings, the pressure now toward the one service with the sanction in its favour in the morning led to 'rump evensongs' as a residue in the evenings. In parishes where evening services, with special emphasis on preaching, and with

[1] Unpublished memorandum quoted by John Wenham in circular to friends calling for the foundation of 'An Evangelical Research Centre' in April 1959.

[2] I doubt if others would have yielded this claim to evangelicals, who were always poor on daily offices, on using the set psalms, on saints' days, and on keeping Lent, etc. But evangelicals thought they were conforming to the 'spirit' of the Book even where they were in breach of the letter. So did others of course. It was only a question of what was 'spirit' and what 'letter'. Evangelicals *did* have a good point over the Thirty-Nine Articles.

[3] In the 1940s and 1950s, no lay person but a few specially authorized, somewhat clericalized lay readers could administer the cup, and none the bread at all. Nor were there many 'NSM's' around. Often a clergyman did both elements on his own to 100 or more communicants. The rules were not changed till 1970.

young people present who went on to youth fellowships and other activities, were a major feature of Sundays and of building up the church, then a move to the parish communion could only be viewed as disadvantageous.

(iv) the crowding young children into the Parish Communion meant, to evangelical critics, both that the preaching was short and interrupted, and that children were being confirmed younger and younger in order to enable them to communicate.

(v) there were also suspicions of some doctrinal and ceremonial accoutrements, and the uncritical sponsorship of *Parish and People* in the 1950s of much 'shallow and romantic Pelagianism' helped evangelicals know to keep clear of the whole enterprise![1]

The upshot is a picture in the late 1950s and early 1960s where Prayer Book services were followed fairly closely on Sundays, with communion at 8 a.m., and possibly after another service once or twice a month, and Morning and Evening Prayer at the hallowed times of 11 and 6.30. Children were probably 'dropped' into a Sunday School during morning service time, though there was a visible growth of 'family services' either in place of Morning Prayer, or (perhaps more frequently) before it.

True evangelical parishes had, at communion, a readily distinguishable liturgical ethos. The following were most notable:

(i) usually the full ten commandments were read.[1]

(ii) there was no server (and no mixed chalice, no washing of the hands, and no elaborate ablutions).

(iii) the priest stood at North Side, in accordance with the rubric, and wore surplice hood and scarf in accordance with the Canons.

(iv) there was no turning East for the Creed.

(v) leavened bread was used, in accordance with the rubric.

(vi) there were no candles, no frontal, burse or veil in 'seasonal colours', and no genuflecting, elevation of the elements, or ringing of bells.

(vii) there was usually a short sermon.

At Morning and Evening Prayer the distinguishing notes were fewer, though the not turning East for the Creed was still almost unique to evangelicals, and the length and character of the preaching were usually distinctive also. Lectionaries were honoured in the breach far more than by other churchmen. So the matter stood in the early 1960s. But events brewing up off-stage were due soon to force a gale of change through many such parishes.

[1] The quotation is from Michael Ramsey in 'The Parish Communion' in *Durham Essays and Addresses* (SPCK, 1956). A fuller treatment of the Robinsonian and kindred kinds of 'romantic' notions will be found in my *The End of the Offertory: An Anglican Study* (Grove Liturgical Study no. 14, 1978).

[2] This was a point of honour among evangelicals, though they frequently overlooked the point that large numbers of their worshippers never came to an '8 o'clock', and thus either did not receive communion or stayed to a staying behind rite which began 'Ye that truly . . .'. Thus the large proportion may never or rarely ever have heard the ten commandments read.

3. TEXTUAL REVISION

With the benefit of hindsight, we all now know that in the late 1950s and early 1960s genuine textual revision of the liturgy was becoming a serious issue. However, it did not break surface much, and I have suggested in the last chapter that the average parish and parishioner did not take it very seriously at the time. In fact revision was being consciously brought into line with the progress of the proposed Prayer Book (Alternative and Other Services) Measure. This went through the Church Assembly in July 1964, and through Parliament in March 1965, and came into force on 1 May 1966.[1] The Liturgical Commission had some texts prepared from the first half of the 1960s, but did not publish them till December 1965.[2]

At this point, whether I like it or not, the story becomes somewhat personal, and has inevitably to be told in the first person singular. For from the Commission's inauguration in 1955 through to 1964 there were no persons on the Commission to which the evangelical constituency could relate.[3] This arose through a variety of causes, no doubt. It included the known policy of Archbishop Fisher.[4] It included the observed lack of interest by evangelicals in reform and revision of the liturgy. It may even have included a supposition that evangelicalism was sufficiently well represented, when to evangelical eyes it seemed not. But it was the case.

Early in 1964 John Wenham wrote an article, originally for publication, in which he said that evangelicals were generally opposed to most proposed changes in the public life of the Church of England, but this was not because they were negative in principle, but because they were excluded from all the official commissions which proposed such changes, and thus had no influence on the issues.[5] On reflection he sent the article not to the press, but to the two archbishops. They took the point—it may prove to have been a crisis moment in the life of the Church of England—and asked him in reply to suggest names which would carry confidence. What he sent back I do not know, but it must have included my name, and in June 1964 I was invited on to the Liturgical Commission.[6] I first attended a meeting in September 1964, when I discovered Series 2 Burial services at the point of completion, Series 2 Communion at an early stage of drafting, and a debate starting

[1] See my *Recent Liturgical Revision in the Church of England* (Grove Booklet on Ministry and Worship no. 14, 1973 and ^{2}1984), hereafter called Booklet 14.

[2] See Booklet 14, pp.18-19.

[3] Whilst the list included one or two such as Cyril Bowles (who was principal of Ridley Hall until 1962) it did not touch the constituency described in the last chapters.

[4] That is, there was a theory that unanimity was built into the composition of Commissions. If this *was* the case, even without evangelicals the Commission before 1964 proved more restive and in more internal conflict than the principle would suggest.

[5] This had been particularly pointed up by the publication of the Anglican-Methodist Scheme in 1963, with four Methodist dissentients but an Anglican consensus—on semi-catholic grounds!

[6] The original letter to me from Archbishop Ramsey said that the desire was that membership 'should both enlist liturgical knowledge and also sufficiently represent varieties of theological outlook . . .'. It was clear that I was in the latter category!

on how or whether the Liturgical Commission would or should be involved with the editing and presentation of Series 1 services. The Archbishop of York (Dr. Coggan) vacated the chair, almost within minutes of my arrival, and was succeeded by Ronald Jasper. I thus counted my time of the Commission to begin from the start of Ronald Jasper's chairmanship.

It was clear that in the first instances all I could do was to identify the doctrinal questions which I found most difficult to accept in the drafts in front of the Commission, and, if necessary, dissent over them. In the first stages of getting aboard the progress of a very learned and determined Commission in full swing, there was no chance of getting my own positive concerns on to the agenda at an early point.[1] I was engaged in what felt like a last-ditch response.

In this squeeze, I identified to myself the following four immediate priorities:

(i) I would not put my signature to any word which I could not defend, or, as officiant at a service, could not in conscience say. Even optional items had to be agreeable to the scriptures and usable by all major streams in the Church of England.

(ii) For the first round of revision, already in full swing, I would *not* stick my toes in immovably over matters of preference—however strongly I might *prefer* another form. I would thus be able to go with the general thrust of revision, and would take responsibility for commending it to my 'constituency', even where I could have preferred it otherwise.

(iii) My first (chronologically first) doctrinal sticking point was going to be petitions for the departed.

(iv) My second sticking point was going to be eucharistic oblation.

Having come to a reasonably settled mind on the first two principles, I found myself immediately facing the third in the draft report for Series 2 Burial. I evaded the problem by asking that, as I had not been present during the compiling of the rite, I might be left off the list of signatories and thus not to take the Commission back to square one, nor have to dissent without having the issues debated (both of which alternatives would have been difficult).[2]

Then we came to Series 2 Communion. The draft intercessions for this also included petitions for the departed, but the great centre of problems was the eucharistic prayer. We had the 1549-type petition for consecration ('that they may be unto us his body and blood'), an Hippolytan-type oblation in the anamnesis ('we offer unto thee this

[1] Thus, to take an instance, I was in no position to urge a move to more modern language.

[2] See Booklet 14, p.19, footnote 1. For a disucussion of the actual principles involved see the booklet cited lower down, *The New Communion Service—Reasons for Dissent* (Church Book Room Press, 1966).

bread and this cup'), and no special emphasis upon the atonement or the theological connection between the cross and the eucharist whatsoever—a staggering departure from Cranmer's rite. On my own principles I had to reckon that I *could* say 'may be unto us', that I could *not* dissent over the lack of a theological emphasis I desired, but that I would *have* to dissent over the oblation.

In June 1965 the Commission was told to present all its materials for publicaltion in a projected report, *Alternative Services: Second Series,* which was duly published in December 1965, as part of the run up to the beginning of the alternative services era, starting on 1 May 1966. The Commission was not ready in June 1965 to agree its eucharistic rite, so a 'Draft Order' was included in the report. I was free to say I did not accept the various parts to which I objected, and I also had a chance to take soundings. So when the Liturgical Conference in February 1966 gave members of the Church Assembly the chance to say they wanted the new communion service quickly, I was able to take steps to see the how my 'constituency' thought on the doctrinal issues.[1] Clearly the Commission was going to have to act in a hurry.

Sure enough, the Commission finished the text at the end of March 1966. Sure enough, I was driven into dissent. Sure enough, no else on the Commission stood with me. And it was clear I had to take my grievance to the Church Assembly and to the country. So I wrote a hasty booklet, *The New Communion Service—Reasons for Dissent*[2], and sent it to all Assembly members. Although the booklet was attacked by Commission members in the Convocations, yet suddenly it proved that the House of Laity held a whip hand and they were going to stand with me.

This development had caught the Assembly platform unprepared. In the House of Laity elections in Autumn 1965 a large number of evangelicals had been returned, and the fact had not been noted in a public way until some time after. But in May 1966 the *First Series* services had been passed in the Convocations under the Alternative Services Measure, and had been sent on to the House of Laity.[3] The Laity debated them on 10 June 1965. A grand row arose over the 1928 Confirmation service, in almost universal use amongst the bishops. The House of Laity denied this rite its necessary two-thirds majority, largely because evangelicals objected to the basing of the rite upon the (untypical) Acts 8 passage. A shock ran through the upper echelons of

[1] Particularly, there was a conference of younger evangelical clergy at Swanwick at the beginning of March and I took thorough soundings there, without giving any guidance as to areas which were concerning me. The findings were published in *The New Communion Service—Reasons for Dissent.*

[2] This was published by the Church Book Room Press on 29 April 1966, the same day that the Commission's report on the completion of *Second Series* communion was published. It was also published in *The Churchman* Vol. 80, no. 2 (Summer 1966).

[3] Before the formation of the General Synod the Houses met and considered liturgical texts separately, with the Clergy sending amended texts on to the Laity. See Booklet 14, p.19, and especially footnote 3.

the Church of England, a new force with synodical clout had suddenly appeared on the scene. Similar debates were held in September and November 1966 over the *First Series* Burial and Communion services, and the one-third blocking vote was not quite reached as unprecedented numbers turned out to vote in answer to an unofficial 'whip' to support the rites.[1]

After this divisive experience, the house of Laity determined to teach the convocations that unitive ways through difficulties must be found, and the offending oblation of the eucharistic elements was changed in the *Second Series* material.[2] Whilst the Convocations still did not get the message squarely in relation to *Second Series* Burial service, the general principle was slowly established.[3] This in turn greatly affected the dynamics of the Liturgical Commission—although I was but one person on the Commission, yet it was clear that my 'constituency' was much stronger than my lone presence indicated, and the Commission itself had best not get itself into a division as between anglo-catholics and evangelicals again.[4]

In fact, life got very much easier from then on. In the writing of the eucharistic prayer for Series 3 communion the chairman involved Kenneth Ross (vicar of All Saints, Margaret Street) and me together, and we were able to reach an agreement which made the whole text look more clearly biblical than had Series 2. The question of petitions for the departed in both the eucharist and the funeral services was greatly helped by two factors:

(i) the publication of *Prayer and the Departed* by the Doctrinal Commission in 1970, and

(ii) a quite untrumpeted victory over the lawyers, who had originally instructed the Commission that every prayer which might be used in a service must be in print in the authorized rite, but were later forced to concede that anything authorized by General Synod *was* authorized in whatever form it took, and a rite might well include a rubric which said *'Other suitable words may be used'*.

Above all, by 1970 evangelicals had proved to the hilt that they wanted new rites, and that the Dix' description of them just did not fit. Arthur Couratin had once said to me 'Evangelicals will always have, and will always use, 1662: anglo-catholics must therefore have a new rite

[1] The *First Series* Burial and Communion services were opposed by the evangelicals in the House of Laity for almost exactly the same reasons as those which led me to dissent from the equivalent *Second Series* services.

[2] See Booklet 14, pp.24-27. See also the Keele Statement (§68) in the Appendix on pp.22-23.

[3] Not only did the Commission get the message (see next sentence above), but the General Synod from 1970 onwards generally acted on the same basis.

[4] The tendency after this was for the Commission to satisfy itself that 'representative' people on the Commission were happy about texts in their own persons, and ready to 'sell' them to their own constituencies. I always viewed this readiness to 'sell' (as the obverse side of the coin of readiness on matters of principle to dissent.

which leans a bit towards them'. I consistently denied the premise of this, and was thus able to deny the conclusion. By 1970, history in the parishes had reinforced my veracity in so doing.

The actual progress of textual revision went on through the 1970s with far less public conflict over these doctrinal issues, because they were being sorted out amicably in advance on the Commission or on the Revision Committees of Synod, and in July and November 1979 the whole package of ASB services was authorized in General Synod with hardly an opponent. A genuine *modus vivendi* of catholics and evangelicals had emerged. Evangelicals could even take initiatives, and the charismatic strand was not without influence.[1] Clearly evangelicals had emerged from their own defensiveness and were keen to play a creative part in the production of new forms.

There remained one blemish on this fair scene, not revealed to the public till after the ASB was launched. Hugh Craig and I were driven into dissent on the Liturgical Commission over a form of absolution of a penitent in the report GS472 published in December 1980. The whole dreary round of the various stages of 1966 and 1967 started to repeat itself, and finally the rite blew itself out in February 1983. Evangelicals in General Synod had not been tested since 1970 as to whether they could raise a blocking one-third in any House of Synod, but they could and they did.[2] Perhaps memories which had forgotten 1966-7 needed some refreshing . . .

[1] For instance, considerable account was taken of charismatics in the provision of *Ministry to the Sick* (ASB 70, 1983)—see Grove Worship Series no. 84, *Liturgy for the Sick: The New Church of England Services,* pp.18-24.

[2] See Grove Liturgical Study no. 39, my *Latest Liturgical Revision in the Church of England 1978-1984,* pp.32-3.

4. LEARNING FROM OTHERS

The 1960s and early 1970s saw evangelicals learning not only to involve themselves in the use of new official texts, but also being ready to learn from others about other features of worship. This is part of the message of the Keele Congress—that they could now see that others had insights and principles which they would be wise to learn, and in many cases adopt.[1] If this chapter is short it is yet highly significant, as its contents are illustrative of the emergence from the ghetto. Two separate but connected areas are chosen.

(i) 'Westward' position

In the late 1940s and early 1950s some *avant garde* spirits of the parish communion type started to go behind the communion tables to preside at communion. Evangelicals were so used to rallying to 'North Side' in order to obviate the perils of Eastward position—and also to continue their stance as those most truly loyal to the rubrics of the BCP—that, when they first noticed the Westward position, they viewed it as an outflanking move to nudge them away from North Side. William Leathem, the vicar of St. John's Harborne, Birmingham, who rebuilt that church with war damage money in the early 1950s, was thought to have been the only evangelical who ever ventured to the Westward position in that decade—and he forfeited a CPAS grant for a curate by so doing.[2] CPAS and Church Society both published in 1963 works of some proportion which, whilst solidly defending 'North Side' and insistently attacking Eastward position, also in passing opposed Westward.[3] It is sad to reflect that the persons concerned were not only giving the wrong answer—they were giving it to the wrong question. What they should have been asking was 'What is the right relationship between the table and the people?' when in fact they asked 'What is the right position of the officiant at the table?'. So they took no steps towards the reordering of churches—how could they when communion itself was not central to church life?—and concentrated on the restricted question.

Yet from 1963 onwards the younger elements of the Eclectics Society were burrowing away to disturb this stance. In 1966 CPAS changed its criterion for giving grants for curates, and in 1967 the Keele Congress declared 'We commend consideration of the westward position'.[4] Ten

[1] 'We . . . hope to learn truths held by others to which we have hitherto been blind, as well as to impart to others truths held by us and overlooked by them.' (*Keele '67,* paragraph 84 (in the 'Unity' section)—cf. paragraph 65 in the appendix here).

[2] CPAS grants for curates were subject to this test, not particularly because the Society wished to be obnoxious, but because an *external* test (North Side) was far easier to apply than an *internal* one about details of belief, and had more evident justice about it.

[3] J. A. Motyer, A. M. Stibbs, J. R. W. Stott, *Why I value North Side Position* (Falcon Books, 1963), and A. Bennett *Table and Minister* (Church Book Room Press, 1963).

[4] See *Keele '67,* paragraph 78.

years later at Nottingham the president of the eucharist naturally and rightly took Westward position. Others by their practice had posed the question and evangelicals came to give the right answer—and began also to see the more fundamental question which underlay it. They are generally still being slow in answering *that* one right . . .

(ii) Weekly Communion

There has always been some dim inkling among evangelicals that to provide communion merely for those able to come at 8 a.m. on a Sunday morning was inadequate. Many evangelical parishes in the 1950s offered 'staying behind' celebrations after Morning or Evening Prayer on one or more Sundays of the month.[1] But by the early 1960s this was in turn giving way to the more corporate pattern of a 'main service communion', again perhaps once a month in the morning and once a month in the evening. The idea behind this was that the 'staying behind' use catered for an individualistic pietism, whereas gathering the church for a main service of communion gave expression to the true corporateness of the church. There were—and are—considerable difficulties about this in practice (as the concept is rarely taught or urged upon the congregation, and so there is often an air of surprise or indifference ('oh, it's communion this week') among them). But the Keele Congress, rather to its own surprise, took the full-blown Parish Communion people seriously, despite all the qualifications.[2] They agreed: 'We determine to work towards the practice of a weekly celebration of the sacrament as the central corporate service of the church . . .'[3] There can have been few present who actually experienced this pattern at the time, and there has been much nervousness about it since.[4] But a very significant public stand had been taken.

The emergence from the ghetto has enabled evangelicals to be undefensive about being sacramentalist. Others had for a century or more practised what seemed to evangelicals to be a false sacramentalism, and this had undoubtedly led to a reaction into a false anti-sacramentalism. Keele specifically renounced this[5], and, although some genuine pastoral and evangelistic reasons have also continued to weigh against the parish communion concept, yet in general the point is accepted at the level of theory. It is in the outworking that evangelicals have been slow to act.

[1] I wrote about this more fully in my *Patterns of Worship* (Grove Booklet on Ministry and Worship no. 9, 1972 and 1975) p.7.

[2] The 'qualifications' are set out on pp.7-8 above.

[3] *Keele '67,* paragraph 76.

[4] See the Nottingham Statement F3(c).

[5] 'Polemics at long range have at times in the past led us into negative and impoverishing "anti"-attitudes (anti-sacramental, anti-intellectual, *etc.*) from which we now desire to shake free.' (*Keele '67,* paragraph 84, in the 'Unity' section).

5. EVANGELICAL INITIATIVES

If a visitor had asked in 1960 what worshipping practices were wholly distinctive to evangelicals (leaving aside the ceremonial sticking-points), the most likely answer would have been the evangelistic service and, perhaps, the midweek prayer meeting. The former of these was a popular event, paralleled by the Sunday evening gospel service at the local Brethren Hall, with well-known hymns and a clearly evangelistic sermon, seeking for actual conversion.[1] Its presupposition was that the non-churchgoers had sufficient church background to be invited to a service in church, and would be unembarrassed once they came. It still can be found in some areas, but the presuppositions are harder to make stick except in certain parts of smoother suburbia.

The informal prayer meeting was wholly distinctive to evangelicals, because no-one else dreamed of extemporary prayer.[2] The Liturgical Movement had certainly not got that far. But evangelicals met in church halls, sang hymns from *Golden Bells,* or some other unchurchy equivalent, had the Bible expounded, and prayed together and aloud for the needs of the parish. There was little notion in those days that this kind of meeting could get imported into the liturgy on Sundays, but something very distinctive and very powerful did exist.[3]

I have already suggested in chapter 2 that in general there was a defensiveness about the use of the Prayer Book services, and initiatives could not easily be expected there. However, a sample of areas of initiatives which had been taken in the decade since gives not only a startling range of creativity, but also further reveals an escape from defensiveness.

(a) Hymnody

The Church Book Room Press produced what with hindsight looked like the last Victorian hymnbook, *The Anglican Hymnbook,* in 1965. It did include 'Tell out, my soul' by Dudley-Smith, but in general its contents were much-loved Wesleyan and Victorian hymns and music. This replaced the previous evangelical collection, *The Hymnal Companion to the Book of Common Prayer,* edited by E. H. Bickersteth in 1870. (Parishes around such evangelicals would be using *Hymns Ancient and Modern (Revised),* if broad or central, and *The English Hymnal,* if somewhat higher). The first genuine new initiative had been taken in the late fifties by the 'Twentieth Century Church Light Music Group', associated with the names of Patrick Appleford and Timothy Beaumont, and by no means evangelical. But in the 1960s evangelicals started to come up fast. The advent of Christian music groups produced a need for new

[1] Whereas the Brethren pattern was often the invariable Sunday evening use, Anglicans would offer it, say, once a month or once a quarter, and issue special invitations to non-churchgoers to come.

[2] When a greater than usual number of evangelicals came together on my ordination retreat in 1961 and asked our ordaining bishop if we could have an extemporary prayer meeting and invite all the ordinands to it, he replied that this would be 'divisive'.

[3] It provided a very strong contrast with the rest of the Church of England, where midweek meetings would either be formal eucharists for saints' days (and it was only in the mid-60s that, following the Pope, these came in the *evening*—until then, for fasting reasons they were in the early morning)—or would be social gatherings like whist drives.

kinds of lyric and music, and first efforts in this direction were found in *Youth Praise,* of which 'I' was published by Falcon in 1966, and 'II' in 1969. The collection included, unbelievably(!), guitar chords—guitars were not see in church until around 1965. It also included, in 'YP II', new renderings of psalms into metrical, but unrhyming, verse for singing to standard hymn-tunes.[1] And this in turn led to the team going on to produce in 1973 *Psalm Praise,* in which the whole Psalter was rendered into the same style of metrical unrhyming verse.[2] The team stayed together, with minor changes, and their latest product is *Hymns for Today's Church* in 1982.[3] Here a whole hymnbook has been produced on the basis of addressing God as 'you', and a thorough programme of retouching well-known hymnody to make it conform to this pattern has been carried through.[4] The evangelicalism of the 1960s is evident on every page—it is the same team, with much of their own creative writing to offer, which produced the earlier books.[5] There is an awareness of the charismatic upsurge which has arisen since they started work, and they include a 'Song Section' with 30 items in it. These draw upon the antediluvian CSSM choruses ('Give me joy in my heart'), upon the writings of the team themselves ('There's no greater name than Jesus' by Michael Baughen), and upon the charismatic sources of the 1970s (e.g. 'Bind us together, Lord', and various Jimmy Owen's titles). But the book if clearly intended for a more formal use, with only this passing nod to the choruses.

(b) Family Services

Whilst the hymn-writing has had a wide potential usefulness, it has flourished in association with one of its most obvious outlets—the 'Family Service'. This is found in a supplementary role to morning worship, before Morning Prayer, or after it, or even (as in the parish I attended in the 1960s) at the same time as it, from well before 1960. However, the trends in the 1960s were towards a family service as the main diet of Sunday morning, it not every week then at stated intervals. The Keele reflections on this stand nearer to what evangelicals were actually doing than does the statement on weekly communion.[6] And

1 See *Youth Praise* Book 2 nos. 160-169. Perhaps the most notable of these has been 'I waited patiently for the Lord' (Psalm 40) by Michael Baughen.

2 *Psalm Praise* was published by Falcon (CPAS).

3 Published by Hodder and Stoughton, and containing over 600 items. The editors of *Youth Praise* had been Michael Baughen, Richard Bewes, and (music) David Wilson. An expanded team edited *Psalm Praise*. Now a much larger team was headed up by the first of these, with Michael Saward as chairman of a words committee (which included Richard Bewes), and David Wilson of a music committee.

4 The whole philosophy of this is defended by another member of the team, Christopher Idle, in Grove Worship Series no. 81, *Hymns in Today's Language* (Grove Books, 1982).

5 They offer not just linguistic 'touching up', but also doctrinal improvement! Thus in Bright's hymn 'And now, O Father, mindful of the love' the lines which evangelicals could not sing were altered. Thus 'for, lo, between our sins and their reward/we set the passion of thy Son our Lord.' became 'for, set between our sins and their reward,/we see the cross of Christ, your Son, our Lord.'! The editors defended this as bringing 'controversial language into the reconciling tradition of the Church of England's "Rite A" order' (Words Preface, third page).

6 See the Keele Statement paragraphs 79-80.

the 1960s saw much work on producing a liturgical outline for such a family service for national use. Michael Botting records how Michael Cole approached him in 1966, and a committee same together, and started consultation up and down the country. As a result CPAS published an outline in Spring 1967 on a folding card.[1] Some parishes started to bind the form of service in with local collections of hymnody and choruses, and CPAS went on in 1971 to produce *Family Worship,* a more substantial paperback book which made wide provision of this sort, and in theory meant that only one book was needed by the worshippers. The family service was experimenting not only with guitars, quizzes and special activities, the use of the overhead projector, drama, and other means of activity involving the congregation, it was also often working at separate instruction for different age-groups within the service, thus swallowing up old-fashioned Sunday Schools. (A vast increase in redesigning premises has gone on alongside and assisted these developments). Michael Botting also produced in 1973 *Teaching the Families* (CPAS).

(c) Baptismal Discipline

Because evangelicals were those in the Church of England with the clearest concept of mission in the 1960s, they were also those with the deepest doubts about indiscriminate infant baptism.[2] Michael Botting, mentioned above, was involved from his earliest days at St. Matthew's Fulham, where he was instituted in 1964, in devising a programme of baptismal discipline.[3] He was not necessarily the first, but he became one of the most notable, not least because the St. Matthew's discipline was one of the tightest in the country. The theory of such discipline was widespread, and it came through in the Keele Statement, which called the existent practice a 'scandal' and urged the need for 'a theologically-inspired national practice of baptismal discipline'. Whilst others have slowly come to share this conviction the pioneering belonged to evangelicals, and their impact is now very wide.[4]

[1] The consultation was conducted especially through the Eclectics Society, the agency of the younger evangelical clergy who were intent on getting out of the ghetto and taking pastoral initiatives. The text is notable as it addressed God as 'you', and was thus in 1967 ahead of all other liturgical texts in the country.

[2] They had doubts of course about baptizing infants at all, but were determined to work to a biblical rationale of it, and of the limits of it. They also had doubts about the Prayer Book language about 'regeneration' (see the Keele Statement, paragraph 71), though it was this very character of what they said at baptisms which was pricking their consciences about the qualifications of the candidates.

[3] His *Twenty Questions on Baptism,* a first attempt to help parents understand why some limits should be placed upon who could be infant candidates, was publsihed by CPAS in 1964, three years after he went to the parish. The EFAC series on 'Christian Foundations', published by Hodder, included in 1966 Geoffrey Hart's *Right to Baptize* (which drew out biblical principles pointing to a discipline, but failed to apply them rigorously).

[4] My own *Baptismal Discipline* (Grove Booklet on Ministry and Worship no. 3, 1972) went through two editions in five years and has long been out of print. Ted Pratt's pamphlet *Thinking about Baptism,* which conveys the message to parents who enquire, has sold tens of thousands (first published by Grove Books in 1977). Meanwhile General Synod has passed a motion asking for the conditions on which infants are accepted for baptism should be re-examined. So has Lima.

6. CHARISMATICS AND EVANGELICALS

In the Church of England the charismatic movement grew out of the evangelical wing of the Church, (initially in the early sixties) but then distanced itself for a while.[1] In the mid-seventies a *rapprochement* began, and it came to an honest junction of the two strands at the Nottingham Congress in April 1977.[2] There is no doubt at all about the creativity and the undefensive character of the charismatic strand, though there *has* been doubt among other evangelicals as to whether charismatics were sufficiently bothered by questions of doctrinal accuracy, or sufficiently critical of all the anglo-catholic practices they were ready to adopt. In broad terms, however, it has been possible since 1977 to call oneself 'evangelical-cum-charismatic'.

In my own experience this reflects not only where many individuals would have to place themselves on the map (certainly it is true of many ordinands), but also where many parishes have reached corporately. Many evangelical parishes, strong and growing in the early seventies, have nevertheless found themselves both adopting the songs of the charismatic movement, and also laying emphasis on a healing ministry, or on full lay participation, which were due in an intangible way to charismatic influences. Parishes can be found which say 'we have prospered on a traditional evangelical programme, moving gently into modern-language worship and fuller participation by the people, but we think God has something more for us'. They do not then have to be in touch with existing charismatic parishes to enter upon a more full-blooded charismatic kind of programme—of openness, prayer counselling, use of 'tongues' or 'prophency', establishment of elderships, etc.[3]

The upshot of these moves is that the charismatic and the evangelical are often hard to distinguish nowadays. Enough old-fashioned evangelicals remain around for there to be a 'constituency', but the growth in numbers, the blurring of distinctions, the impatience with labels, and the opportunity to influence the rest of the Church of England, have all conspired to make the 'party' less easy to find and identify. Perhaps the most significant factor is the last one mentioned—as 'parties' sense that their message is wanted by many others than themselves, they lose the defensiveness so often noted above, and begin to try to make that impact. Worship meanwhile becomes more 'open', people become a people of God within it, and a warm fellowship develops. Possibly the evangelical-cum-charismatic concept and practice of fellowship is now one of the most clearly distinguishing features of the joint strand.

[1] I have traced some of this effect in my two writings on the charismatic movement Grove Booklet on Ministry and Worship no. 77, *Encountering Charismatic Worship* (1977); and the official report (which I largely drafted), *The Charismatic Movement in the Church of England* (CIO, 1981).

[2] See my *Anvil* article cited on page 3 above.

[3] The distinctive features of charismatic worship are listed in my booklet 77 noted in footnote 1 above, and I do not attempt to be exhaustive here. I use quotation marks round mention of two 'gifts of the Spirit' as I consider that the exegetical and pastoral review of all that is involved in these 'gifts' is not yet complete.

7. THE GROUP FOR RENEWAL OF WORSHIP

It seems appropriate for Tract no. 90 to lift a corner of the veil which normally obscures the membership of the Group for the Renewal Of Worship, and includes a summary of its work. Such a summary comes inevitably out of the centre of the Group, and cannot pretend to objectivity.

In 1961 I was invited to join a 'Latimer House Liturgy Group' which was being launched as part of the whole Latimer House project. The Group was chaired initially by Richard Coates, the first warden, for a short time by Jim Packer, when he succeeded in 1962 to the wardenship, and then, from 1964 onwards, by Roger Beckwith, who was then Librarian. In 1971 I became chairman, and in 1976 the Group became independent of Latimer House, and took on its new title 'G-R-O-W'.

The Group's first project was to write a confirmation service (partly in reaction against the Commission's work of 1959), and the Eclectics invited joint work on a baptism service. The work was published in 1967[1], and, although after a minor tussle the language was still in 'thou' form, many points of principle were illustrated in the introduction and texts, and some of these did affect Series 3 baptism and confirmation services in the late seventies.[2] The Group itself addressed itself to responding to the publication of Series 2 communion, and trying to lay down guidelines for its revision to become Series 3. In the process two different policies emerged, and these were in conflict with each other:

(i) the definitive evangelical response: this view required a very thoroughly tested alternative text with doctrinal and other introduction, which would both enable evangelicals to see how the Group was responding to the official texts (and thus hearten the dispirited), and also give the Liturgical Commission and the Synod some clear alternatives on which to reflect. This response was indeed made in respect of the eucharist.[3]

(ii) the provisional, more lightweight, and undefensive response: this view looked for publications which were not necessarily representative of evangelicals at large, nor even agreed by the whole Group, but which started to open the debate in as many fields as possible. In fast-moving times the provisional was seen as the right form of response. This view was sufficiently strong on the Group in 1967 to lead to a most imaginative publication, *Eucharist for the Seventies.*[4] This was in modern language, with

[1] R. T. Beckworth, C. O. Buchanan, K. W. F. Prior (eds.) *Baptism and Confirmation* (Latimer Monograph 2, Marcham Manor Press, 1967).

[2] Particularly the concept of a single rite for baptizing adults and infants together.

[3] R. T. Beckwith and J. E. Tiller (eds.) *Holy Communion and its Revision* (Latimer Monograph 3, Marcham Manor Press, 1971). This also included a 'modenized 1662'. The 'definitive' concept had been gently abandoned and the introductory chapters were signed only by the two editors.

[4] This was published as a cheap 'Grove Booklet' kind of publication by 'Northwood Christian Book Centre', the forerunner of Grove Books. The major responsibility for it was taken by two editors, Christopher Byworth and Trevor Lloyd. The second offprinting of the text came from Grove Books, and copies are still available of the offprint.

very full congregational participation, and revolutionary 'shape'. Demand was such that in 1969 and 1971 offprints of the text without the introduction were made for the actual use (sometimes in informal contexts) which had developed overnight for the rite.

In 1971 the Group, slightly reorganized, committed itself to following the second of these two policies.[1] From that was born the series of Grove Booklets on Ministry and Worship, beginning on the last day of 1971. The booklets orginated within the Group, or were commissioned by it. Authors took responsibility individually for their own writings. Evangelicals were writing experimentally, and writing to have an impact on the whole church. The booklets were as often as not unbothered about *texts,* but instead were concentrating on pastoral use of services, presentation of liturgy, teaching in the context of worship, and parish liturgical policy. However, the authorization of Series 3 communion in Autumn 1972 (for publication in January 1973) occasioned special publications which virtually stole the publishing field from all others, and gave a good financial undergirding to the publications for the next three years or so.[2]

In 1975 the monthly booklets incorporated a once-a-quarter more weighty 'Grove Liturgical Study', and these specialist monographs have been designed to provide for the whole field of liturgical study, even when an author or editor was not an evangelical. A general oversight of the titles has been exercised by the Group, but the authors have been untrammelled by any doctrinal or other requirements. *News of Liturgy* started at the same time as the Liturgical Studies and reaches its tenth anniversary at the end of 1984 also.

The Group asked itself in 1977 how it ought to respond to the authorization of the Alternative Service Book due in 1980, and devised a plan which reached fruition (against the clock, and only made possible by the adventurous spirit of Collins Liturgical Publications) in *Anglican Worship Today: Collins' Illustrated Guide to the Alternative Service Book 1980.* This was edited by COB, Trevor Lloyd, and Harold Miller (then secretary of the Group), and it provided a completely new pattern of teaching aid to accompany the Church of England' worship book.[3] At the time of writing it has sold around 16000 copies (including many in other parts of the world) and done much to enable thinking lay people to understand comtemporary worship. The Group has had many other spin-offs also, not least in the music area, where Robin Leaver produced in 1980 *Hymns with the New Lectionary,* and in 1982 started editing a quarterly companion to *News of Liturgy—News of Hymnody.* At the time of writing three members of the Group have just produced *Ways of Singing the Psalms,* published also by Collins.

[1] This did not mean that the Group treated the other policy as wholly inappropriate, and my own collections of Anglican liturgies from round the world have been partly intended to illustrate that evangelicals have a role to play in official liturgy-writing.

[2] Along with Booklets 10 and 12 (*A Guide to Series 3* and *The Language of Series 3),* both of which went into two printings very quickly, there were *Collects with the New Lectionary* and *Series 3 for the Family,* which went to four printings.

[3] The team is currently at work on a sister book to *Anglican Worship Today,* and hopes to take the wraps off in the Spring.

APPENDIX: THE TWO STATEMENTS

(a) KEELE (1967). The First National Evangelical Congress (held at the University of North Staffordshire at Keele from 4 to 7 April 1967) produced an agreed 'Statement' endorsed by the plenary sessions of the Congress, 1000 people in all. The Statement (published in *Keele '67* (ed. Philip Crowe) (Falcon Books, 1967)) included six main sections, arising from the six sections of the Congress. Section 5 dealt with worship:

5. The Church and its Worship

Ministry and worship
64. Worship Godward and witness manward together constitute the duty of the whole Church. The ministry of Word and Sacrament in the power of the Holy Spirit enables the body of Christ to understand and receive God's salvation in all its fullness, to respond to respond to God in praise and self-surrender, and to be renewed corporately for its task of mission in the world.

Our failures
65. We acknowledge that in the past we have not achieved these ideals. We have failed to maintain the unity of Word and Sacrament. While rightly exalting preaching, we have underrated the evangelical function of the sacrament of the Lord's Supper as a visible word. We have been suspicious of experimentation and frightened of change, and have tended to individualism. Furthermore, we have been slow to learn from other parts of God's Church.

LITURGICAL REVISION

Attitude to revision
66. Liturgical revision is long overdue. Much as we value the doctrinal basis of the services of 1662, we are not so wedded to their structures, contents or language as not to see the need for new forms. Some of us desire these new forms to be a conservative revision of the present services; some desire services in modern language, and strongly urge the provision of such forms for an experimental period; while others are looking for something much more radical, though retaining the same doctrinal position as 1662. But to all the period of experiment is welcome. No alarms should accompany the loosening of a legal uniformity, although we believe that the ideal of Common Prayer should not be forgotten.

New Testament theology makes the local church corporately responsible for ordering and offering worship aright. The Prayer Book (Alternative and Other Services) Measure gives responsibility to Parochial Church Councils to consent or otherwise to the use of new forms of service in church in a parish. We therefore call on incumbents and Parochial Church Councils to study the proposed services, in order to discharge their biblical and legal responsibility in this matter. The resultant local variations in worship should not cause Christians to take offence when they move from one part of the country to another. Equally, local churches should not give offence by unlawful innovations. We call on all local churches to abide by the present law, even where it seems irksome. We ourselves will seek reform only by lawful means.

Biblical basis
67. The proper basis of liturgical revision is not the practice of the second and third centuries, but the teaching of the Bible applied with reference to contemporary needs and in the light of existing services.

Liturgical commission services
68. We consider that the services presented by the Liturgical Commission have many excellent features structurally, and, in the case of the new Baptism and Confirmation Services, linguistically. However, certain doctrinal points in some of the proposed services cause serious objections. For example: the Initiation Services overvalue Confirmation; the Burial Service fails to express Christian assurance and hope; the Holy Communion service in its present form includes an offering of the bread and the cup to God and explicit petitions for the departed, and contains no adequate reference to the Second Coming.

In the case of Holy Communion, we desire that the service should more clearly affirm its grounding in the once-for-all sacrifice of Christ upon the Cross; it can be spoken of in sacrificial terms only in the sense that it embraces the responsive self-offering of believers in gratitude for Christ's finished work of sin-bearing. We share the longing, voiced on several occasions in the Church Assembly, for liturgy that will be consistently biblical and consequently unifying. We affirm our readiness to enter into dialogue with those from whom we differ, with a view to finding the best way of securing such liturgy.

THE MINISTRY OF THE WORD

Priority of preaching
69. We call on the Church to set the highest standards for the ministry of the Word, to proclaim the whole counsel of God, and to recover an eager expectation of receiving grace through this means. Preaching is the authoritative proclamation of the Word of God, applied by the Spirit demanding decision rather than discussion. We therefore regard the development of techniques of discussion and dialogue for Christian instruction as a useful adjunct to preaching, but not as a substitute for it.

Preaching standards
70. The whole Church must co-operate if the proper function of preaching is to be recovered in our day. Colleges must give deeper and balanced training in theology, communication and psychology. Ministers must dicover the needs of their congregations with a view to relevant preaching. Congregations must set their ministers free to devote themselves to prayer and ministry of the Word. Preachers must avail themselves of every opportunity to improve their preaching.

THE MINISTRY OF THE SACRAMENTS—I. HOLY BAPTISM

Baptism is the sign and seal of covenant-relationship between God and His people.

Infant baptism
71. We affirm our belief in the scriptural foundation of infant baptism, but declare that only the children of parents who profess to be Christians are fit subjects for this rite. Indiscriminate baptism, as commonly practised in England, is a scandal, and is incidentally productive of much of the current divisive reaction against the baptizing of infants. We call now for a theologically-inspired national practice of baptismal discipline.

We must be welcoming to little children, as Jesus was. But we deny the propriety of baptizing the infants of parents who do not profess to be Christians themselves and who cannot promise to bring up their children as Christians. We approve the proposals regarding Christian parenthood and upbringing which are embodied in the Preface to the new Service for Infant Baptism.

In view of the widespread misunderstanding caused by such expressions as 'this child is regenerate', we would welcome their revision, provided that the covenant basis which they express is not lost.

Public baptism
72. We urge that baptism should always be held at public services of the Church, unless there are compelling reasons to the contrary. The baptism liturgies of the Church of England need further revision to enable whole families to be baptized together with one rite.

Confirmation
73. Christian initiation is sacramentally complete in baptism. The confirmation of those baptized as adults should be combined with their baptism, as proposed by the Liturgical Commission. But the declarations of repentance and faith which are made in infant baptism need to be ratified by the child at the age of discretion. This ratification may be accompanied appropriately by the laying on of hands, although this act is not essential to the service.

Admission to Communion
74. We call for further theological study as to whether the age of discretion is always the right time for admission to Holy Communion. Some of us would like the children of Christian families to be admitted as communicants at an early age, provided that there is adequate baptismal discipline.

Rebaptism
74 We reject rebaptism as unscriptural. It is destructive of the sacrament, makes it a sign of our faith rather than of God's grace, and removes its once-for-all character. It is also hurtful to the unity of God's people.

THE MINISTRY OF THE SACRAMENTS—II. HOLY COMMUNION

Its centrality
76. We have failed to do justice in our practice to the twin truths that the Lord's Supper is the main service of the people of God, and that the local church, as such, is the unit within which it is properly administered. This is not to undervalue in any way attendance at other services of the day, but to admit that we have let the sacrament be pushed to the outer fringes of church life, and the ministry of the Word be divorced from it. Small communion services have been held seemingly at random, often more than one a Sunday, and the whole local church seldom or never comes together at the Lord's Table. As individuals we have lacked both a concern that the local church should amend its ways, and also a personal discipline of attendance.

We determine to work towards the practice of a weekly celebration of the sacrament as the central corporate service of the church, and some of us would recommend the use of 'one loaf' (1 Corinthians 10.17) as biblical and symbolic of that corporate unity.

Participation
77. Authorized lay people, in addition to Readers, should assist by reading the lessons, by leading the intercessions, by preaching and by administering both elements.

The Position of the minister
78. We believe that the minister should stand where he may break bread before the people. We commend consideration of the westward position.

THE FAMILY

Family worship
79. We assert out belief that the basic unit of the local church is the family, and that the family at worship together is the ideal for which we should strive. Children should be seen, within the Christian family, as fellow-children of God with their parents. We welcome the continuing growth of family worship as the liturgical threshold by which whole families are introduced to the life of the Church, and thus to Jesus Christ. Non-sacramental family services must not, however, become ends in themselves, but must lead on to participation in the full worship of the Church, including the sacraments.

Family evangelism and fellowship
80. Care must be taken lest this form of evangelism become child-orientated, and teaching consequently childish. The Church must labour in family evangelism, as well as in child-evangelism, although we recognize the importance of the systematic instruction of children. Further, the distinction between adult and child, old and young, in the life of the Church, must not be too rigid. Christian fellowship, objectively expressed and fostered through liturgy, should break down barriers of age, and unite whole families more securely.

(b) **NOTTINGHAM** (1977). The Second National Evangelical Anglican Congress (held at the University of Nottingham from 14 to 18 April 1977) involved 2000 participants. They divided into eighteen subsections, relating to the eighteen chapters in the three preparatory books, *Obeying Christ in a Changing World* (Collins, Fount, 1977). Each participant took part in discussion on six of the eighteen chapters, and helped draft sectional statements. Finally, nine 'subplenaries' amended and agreed the redrafting of the statements undertaken by the authors of the chapters. No section was entitled 'Christian worship', but the most relevant material is found under the headings 'F The Life of the Local Church' (author Trevor Lloyd) and 'Q Christian Beginning' (author George Carey):

F3: Worship
(a) We long for God's Holy Spirit and the Word of God to inspire and control the worship in every church in the country, whatever the tradition or form of service.

(b) We welcome the imaginative reappraisal of the Sunday pattern of worship in many churches.

(c) We are equally divided whether we should reaffirm (Keele Para. 76) that the main church meeting on Sunday should be eucharistic in its worship. In any case, we urge that it should have a considerable amount of time devoted to the promotion of Christian growth among adults and also involve the different gifts and ministries of many members of the congregation in both worship and teaching. The Sunday-morning worship also needs to be such as to encourage families to worship together and to be flexible in pattern and time. We welcome the opportunity for spontaneity in worship and for the exercise of spiritual gifts in worship where practical.

(d) We enjoy our written liturgy and welcome in the Series 3 services the emphasis on joy, freedom, flexibility and congregational involvement. We should like to see these features extended—*e.g.* in providing variety in the intercessions and in the Thanksgiving in Holy Communion (though we do not think alternative Thanksgivings should be designed to cater for docotrinal differences). We commend experimentation with drama, dance, music, movement, colour, furnishings and setting to heighten the awareness and involvement of God's people in true worship.

(e) On the revision of Series 3 Holy Communion in particular, we are concerned lest any revision should give greater weight to the concepts of petition for the departed, eucharistic sacrifice or permanent reservation of the elements. We are also concerned because a number of our brethren believe that these concepts are already emphasized too greatly, so much so that they feel conscientiously unable to use the service without grave misgivings. We would urge that the main focus of the *anamnesis* (the part of the Thanksgiving prayer that turns our attention back to the redeeming work of God in Christ) should be the death of Christ, as it is of the whole 1662 service and as it was in the original text of this part of the Liturgical Commission's Series 3 service, without in any sense wanting to lose the broad doctrinal sweep of the mighty acts of God and of the present realities of Baptism, the Spirit, the Church and the future hope of Christ's coming back again. We reaffirm that intentional verbal ambiguity to bring together mutually contradictory doctrinal positions should not be a principle of liturgical revision.

(f) The Church on earth is marked out by Baptism, which is complete sacramental initiation into Christ and his body. We emphasize that both the outward sign and the inward work of grace are essential to the full benefit of the sacrament. We accept adult Baptism as the theological norm but agree that the children of Christian parents are rightly included as recipients of Baptism and are to be brought up as members of the community. We believe, however, that the practice of indiscriminate Baptism is wrong, because it blurs the distinction between the Church and the world and encourages an understanding of Christianity that verges on a folk religion. We safeguard the font in a parallel manner to the way in which we safeguard the Lord's table. If parents refuse to participate in reasonable educational preparation for Baptism, they must be deemed to have ruled themselves out. In the final assessment of those who complete the course, we urge the utmost charity. We consider that Baptism should always take place within public services unless there are compelling reasons to the contrary. The next stage after Baptism is to come to the Lord's Supper, but it is clear in Scripture that an element of discernment is involved in participating. We urge the church to look again at the Ely report and should like to see: